Living in the Design

Living in the Design

A Sailing Devotional

Dave and Jamie Stadler

ELM HILL

A Division of
HarperCollins Christian Publishing

www.elmhillbooks.com

Living in the Design
A Sailing Devotional

Published in Nashville, Tennessee, by Elm Hill, an imprint of Thomas Nelson. Elm Hill and Thomas Nelson are registered trademarks of HarperCollins Christian Publishing, Inc.

Elm Hill titles may be purchased in bulk for educational, business, fund-raising, or sales promotional use. For information, please e-mail SpecialMarkets@ ThomasNelson.com.

Library of Congress Cataloging-in-Publication Data

Library of Congress Control Number: 2019919039

ISBN 978-1-400329823 (Paperback)
ISBN 978-1-400329830 (eBook)

INTRODUCTION

Using This Book on Land

This book is meant to be enjoyed.

Whether you read it daily, weekly, or whenever you get the chance, please enjoy it.

Whether you read it by a fireplace, at the beach, on a commuter train, or on an airplane, please enjoy it.

Whether you read it alone or with a group of friends, please enjoy it.

However, this book is mostly meant to be enjoyed on the water.

Using This Book Afloat

Time on the water has an effect on people. On our sailboat, *Teleo*, we have seen its effect on our guests and have certainly experienced it firsthand—that palpable soul connection with God's creation out on the water. The silence of sailing and elimination of other worldly distractions provides hours of quality time to connect with others as we share in that creation together. Onboard *Teleo*, we often say that there is no such thing as "we really don't know them well... we only sailed with them once."

This devotional book is designed to strengthen the experience of connecting creation and Creator by drawing out parallels between sailing and God's truth as disclosed in scripture. Key aspects include the following:

- The devotions are for people at any level of faith.
- The devotions can be enjoyed by experienced or beginning sailors.
- You can do these devotions in any order.
- The devotions do not require an expert to lead; however, they can be embellished by those with more Biblical knowledge or sailing knowledge. (Hint: two different people might lead each section.)
- They are short enough to do between tacks on a day sail or as daily time during a long passage.
- For more in-depth study, those at anchor might choose to look up the scriptures in the "For Further Reading" section in their Bibles or on their Bible app such as Bible Gateway.
- While these devotionals can be read individually, they are designed to be discussed in groups. We strongly recommend in groups as that is often how God uses each of us to puzzle out our faith in community.

We hope this little book will further enrich your next sailing adventure and your relationship with the Creator God.

#

TABLE OF CONTENTS

1. Psalm 104 — 1
2. Living in the Design — 3
3. Just Being on a Boat — 7
4. Psalm 102 — 11
5. The Constant Star — 13
6. True North — 17
7. Sea Story from Mark: Who Is This? — 21
8. Keep a Weather Eye — 23
9. Psalm 148 — 27
10. Song Story: It Is Well with My Soul — 29
11. Setting an Anchor — 31
12. Dead Calm — 35
13. Sea Story from Matthew: Walking on Water — 39
14. Waves — 41
15. Tides — 45
16. Psalm 147 — 49
17. Song Story: Amazing Grace — 51
18. The Importance of a Name — 55
19. Running Aground — 59
20. Shortcuts and Grace — 63
21. Teach Them to Yearn — 67
22. Psalm 139 — 71

23. Featured Sea Story: Shipwrecked!   73

24. The Shortest Distance   81

25. Dressed and Ready to Go   85

26. Teamwork   89

27. Psalm 107   93

28. Halyards and Lines   95

29. Rudder   99

30. Evidence of the Invisible   103

31. Psalm 19   107

32. Rules of the Road   109

33. Time to Shorten Sail   113

34. Redemption   117

Acknowledgments   *121*

#

PSALM 104

Bless the Lord, O my soul!
O Lord my God, you are very great!
You are clothed with splendor and majesty,
Covering yourself with light as with a garment,
Stretching out the heavens like a tent,
He lays the beams of His chambers on the waters;
He makes the clouds His chariot;
He rides on the wings of the wind;
He makes His messengers winds,

His ministers a flaming fire.
O Lord, how manifold are your works!
In wisdom have you made them all;
The earth is full of your creatures.
Here is the sea, great and wide,
Which teems with creatures innumerable,
Living things both small and great.
There go the ships, and Leviathan,
which you formed to play in it.

May the glory of the Lord endure forever;
May the Lord rejoice in His works...
I will sing to the Lord as long as I live;
I will sing praise to my God while I have being.
May my meditation be pleasing to Him,
for I rejoice in the Lord...
Bless the Lord, O my soul!
Praise the Lord!

(Psalm 104:1–4, 24–26, 31, 33, 35, ESV)

#

LIVING IN THE DESIGN

A sailboat makes a lousy powerboat ... just try backing into a boat slip under a gusty crosswind. (If you haven't already done so, that tricky maneuver inevitably comes with a crowded marina and lots of armchair spectators.) The sailboat's propeller is fixed and pointed at the stern of the boat. While a powerboat's propeller often pivots in the same direction when in reverse—making backing easier—a sailboat's prop operating astern behaves like a rototiller pulling the boat in a sideways direction, typically to port. All of these things make backing a sailboat, according to one man, like "blowing a Kleenex back into the box."

However, under sail, the story is entirely different. Take the same gusty day. When the sails are hoisted, they flap violently and make a lot of noise, but once a skilled helmsman turns the boat to embrace the wind, the boat heels, digs in, and comes to life. The sideway pressure on the sails push against the rudder and keel, and this produces forward motion. The boat will speed along in the direction it is pointed, solid as a rock. If the sails are trimmed correctly, the helmsman can remove his or her hand from the wheel or tiller and the boat will sail itself. It is doing that for which it is designed.

Sailboats are designed to sail.

Key Scripture

... everyone who is called by my name, whom I created for my glory, whom I formed and made.

(ISAIAH 43:7, ESV)

It is a universal heart question: *Why do I exist?* Isaiah 43:7 tells us straight out: we are created, formed, and made for God's glory! This is our purpose. This is our reason for being.

But what does that mean? So very often we are sailboats living as powerboats. We think our purpose has to do with a "right" job, a perfect home, status, achievements, or even love and family. But that is the world's purpose, and it will come up empty because it does not fit with how we were made. If we have all that, but not the Lord, we will eventually ask: *Is this all there is?*

God places in the human soul a deep desire to live in the design of who we were created to be, and that desire is *only* met in Him. His ordained will for our lives—our own divine sweet spot—only flows out of that. When you accomplish that for which you were created, there is a very special Greek word you are living out—*Teleo*.

Jesus spoke this word on the cross when He accomplished the will of His Father for our salvation. *Teleo... It is finished!* Teleo goes far beyond the end of something. It has to do with a complete fulfillment, a mature perfection, and a wholeness. "The will of the Lord shall prosper in His hand. Out of the anguish of His soul, He shall see light and be satisfied."* When Jesus fulfilled His reason for being on this earth, His soul was satisfied. His reason for being on this earth was you, and your reason for being on this earth is Him.

Discussion

Why did God create you?

What is your divine purpose?

Do you experience a sense of fulfillment in life?

For Further Reading

Psalm 139:13–16, Psalm 16:11, John 19:28–30, *Isaiah 53:10–11

#

JUST BEING ON A BOAT

Believe me, my young friend, there is nothing—absolutely nothing—half so much worth doing as simply messing about in boats.

(KENNETH GRAHAME)

The famous quote above is from the children's book *The Wind in the Willows*. We might beg to differ on his assertion in the literal sense, but ask any sailor at heart, and he or she will confess a pull to simply be on his boat.

The *way* the sailor is on the boat could take on many forms: out for a day sail, on a journey to a destination, anchored in a cove, or even at a dock.

Walk down a dock, and you might see groups of people in the cockpit enjoying each other's company. (In some marinas, these take on an old-fashioned "front porch" feel as neighboring boat owners greet each other while passing by down the "street" of the dock.)

Perhaps he is puttering on his boat working through his task list.

Or maybe she is lounging on the foredeck—reading, napping, relaxing—simply being on her boat.

Key Scripture

Abide in me, and I in you.

(JOHN 15:4A, ESV)

Jesus spoke these words to His closest disciples on the night of His arrest; it was part of His last discourse to them... and through them to us. Again and again, Jesus urges His followers to "abide in me, and I in you."

Abide means to remain or dwell. In John 15, it is a continual intimate union between Christ and His follower. "Abide in my love... these things I have spoken to you, that my joy may be in you, and that your joy may be full."

Who wouldn't want that? When one abides in Jesus, there is a pull to abide in Him more and more—to simply be with Jesus. Abiding does not mean that we walk around with hands folded and eyes closed in pious prayer at all times; rather, we view every moment through God's lens by His Spirit. In short, we practice His presence in whatever we do.

Brother Lawrence was a dishwasher at a monastery during the seventeenth century. Although he worked a menial job (too uneducated to serve as cleric), he enjoyed God's presence right at the kitchen sink. He washed dishes for God's glory, and it showed; visitors traveled in droves to seek his counsel.

One can well imagine Brother Lawrence humbly guiding a young follower with these words: *Believe me, my young friend, there is nothing—absolutely nothing—half so much worth doing as abiding in Jesus.*

Discussion

What are ways you practice the presence of God?

For Further Reading

John 15:1–17, 1 Corinthians 10:31, 1 John 3:24

#

PSALM 102

Of old you laid the foundation of the earth,
And the heavens are the work of your hands.
They will perish, but you will remain;
They will all wear out like garment.
You will change them like a robe,
And they will pass away,
But you are the same,
and your years have no end.

(Psalm 102:25–27, ESV)

#

THE CONSTANT STAR

But I am as constant as the northern star.

(*JULIUS CAESAR* BY SHAKESPEARE)

At sea, the horizon extends all directions with no landmarks to guide the journey. But there *is* a guiding "skymark"—the North Star.

For centuries, sailors have relied on the North Star. Every night, regardless of season, the star appears immoveable above our north pole as the northern sky rotates around it. The outer bowl of the Big Dipper points directly to this star fixed on the handle of the Little Dipper.

The North Star is not only a reliable compass, it also gives the celestial navigator approximate latitude—invaluable out on the open sea. At the north pole, the North Star is positioned directly overhead; at the equator, it shines on the horizon. The navigator can deduce the vessel's latitude through the angle of the North Star.

Other names for the North Star—originating across various cultures and time periods—are Polaris, pole star, steadfast star, fixed star, guiding star, stella maris (sea star), and lodestar (lode means journey or course.)

Navigator's Tip

Your fist held up to the night sky at arm's length is about ten degrees of latitude. Thomas Point Lighthouse in the Chesapeake Bay near Annapolis is at a latitude of 38° 58' 42.3948"N. From that vantage point, the North Star is nearly four fists above the horizon.

Did You Know?

The North Star is not a single star, but a three-star system illuminating as one.

Key Scripture

For I am the Lord, I change not.

(MALACHI 3:6, KJV)

God is our unchangeable North Star. The God of the universe who holds all power in His creative hands yet is all good and the essence of love—it is this God who has declared, "I am the Lord, I change not!"

He is not like us. God is not fickle; He does not change His mind, and He keeps every promise. Nor is He like the rest of nature which buds, blooms, matures, and dies.

Creation is wild and glorious yet all the while changing with a beginning and an end. Even the North Star—which we perceive as an immovable light—is slowly inching across our northern hemisphere. In fact, it will be at its closest to the north pole in 2100. This subtle change is only discernable across centuries. One day our dependable guiding star will move beyond our pole and cease to be a point of reference marking the sky.

But the One who created the cosmos and knows every star by name is the very Father of lights with whom there is no variation or shadow due to change. Our eternal, self-existent God is the same yesterday, today, and forever.

Discussion

Using the North Star as a poetic metaphor or analogy, what characteristics do you see in the North Star that could be used as a metaphor for God?

Do you find God's unchangeable nature reassuring or uncomfortable?

Who or what is your North Star?

Why?

For Further Reading

Numbers 23:19, Isaiah 40:8, James 1:17, Hebrews 13:8

#

TRUE NORTH

The compass was one of the most significant inventions in human history. It allowed navigators numerous options for determining the position of their vessel relative to other things and to sail a course that was the shortest distance possible between two points. Unlike the previous reliance on just the North Star, it was available all day and under any weather conditions.

Despite its advantages, every able navigator knows that a compass reads magnetic north, not true north. True north is the point around which the earth rotates—where all of the lines of longitude converge on a globe and the axis of the globe penetrates the surface. However, the earth has a magnetic field—both at its surface and in its core—which disrupts the compass reading.

Due to this magnetic field, the compass points to magnetic north rather than true north. This is not a fixed distance—while true north remains true, magnetic north does not. The constant motion of liquid within our planet's core changes the position of magnetic north—roughly forty miles per year. Scientists cannot yet predict accurately where it will wander over time. If you set off with a compass to find the North Pole, you may end up 500 miles away.

Nautical charts compensate for this difference by showing both true north (which we sail to) and magnetic north (which our compass reads). In the mid-Atlantic area around the Chesapeake Bay, the difference is currently about eleven degrees of variation.

Did You Know?

The magnetic field at the earth's core is fifty times more intense than the magnetic field at the earth's surface.

Key Scripture

I have stored up Your Word in my heart, that I might not sin against You.

(PSALM 119:11, ESV)

What is the true north for our lives? Modern culture is a confusing compass. While seeking to give direction, it constantly changes those directions: get rich/give back, save the planet/it's all about you, and use your head/follow your heart. And here is the most confusing of all: *truth is whatever is true for you.*

Scripture warns that the world has exchanged truth for a lie, worshipping creation rather than the Creator, and it tells us flat out that the heart is deceitful above all things. So if we can't trust the world's definition of truth, and if we can't even trust our own fickle hearts, we may well ask, "How then can we possibly know the truth?"

The teachings of Jesus are revealing: "I am the way, and the truth, and the life; If you abide in my Word... you will know the truth, and the truth will set you free; when the Spirit of truth comes, He will guide you into all the truth; Your Word is truth" (John 14:6, 8:31–32, 16:13a, 17:17, ESV).

God is our only true north—His very nature is without sin. Like a nautical chart, scripture points us to the character of God and exposes sin. The living and active Word of God teaches, guides, and changes us more and more into the likeness of God.

Discussion

In what ways is God our true north?

How has the world exchanged truth for a lie?

Why do we need the chart of God's Word?

How do we overcome our old nature?

For Further Reading

Romans 1:25, Jeremiah 17:9, 1 Corinthians 1:18–21, Hebrews 4:12, John 17:14–17, Ephesians 4:18–24

\#

SEA STORY FROM MARK: WHO IS THIS?

On that day, when evening had come, He [Jesus] said to them, "Let us go across to the other side."

And leaving the crowd, they took Him with them in the boat, just as He was. And other boats were with Him.

And a great windstorm arose, and the waves were breaking into the boat so that the boat was already filling. But He was in the stern, asleep on the cushion. And they woke Him and said to Him, "Teacher, do you not care that we are perishing?"

And He awoke and rebuked the wind and said to the sea, "Peace! Be still!" And the wind ceased, and there was a great calm.

He said to them, "Why are you so afraid? Have you still no faith?"

And they were filled with great fear and said to one another, "Who then is this, that even the wind and the sea obey Him?" (Mark 4:35–41, ESV)

#

KEEP A WEATHER EYE

It goes without saying: sailboats need wind to sail. Sailors are always on the lookout for wind. They must also try to avoid or prepare for bad weather. In short, a good sailor understands weather.

In ancient times, weather was thought to be almost completely random. Mariners developed certain truisms—such as *red sky at night, sailors delight; red sky at morning, sailors take warning*. They saw the weather patterns but didn't know why it was so.

In modern times, we know many of the underlying factors. For example, differences in temperature cause differences in pressure. Differences in pressure cause air to move from high pressure to low pressure and create wind. Warm air can hold more water than cold air, so as warm air rises and cools, it may produce precipitation. Land heats and cools more quickly than the ocean, so we will always have breezes at the shore. Despite knowing the factors, we can't always predict how the factors will interact and what weather we can expect.

These weather systems are in precise balance to sustain life on earth. Temperature differences across the globe pick up moisture in certain places, while the rotation of the earth distributes it elsewhere. The tilting of the earth on its axis causes seasons to occur in various parts of the earth by time of the year. Rotation causes night and day. While droughts may exist—even for years at a time—history proves rain will eventually return. Even deserts and rain forests are explainable and necessary and remain as such indefinitely. Hundreds of intricate weather processes work together to sustain our life here on earth.

Did You Know?

Jesus quoted these sayings to the Pharisees as He admonished them for knowing how to correctly interpret the skies but not perceiving the signs He had already performed in their presence, signs that pointed to who He was—the Son of God.

Key Scripture

Who is this? Even the wind and the waves obey Him!

(MARK 4:41, NIV)

For as the rain and the snow come down from heaven and do not return there but water the earth, making it bring forth and sprout, giving seed to the sower and bread to the eater, so shall my word be that goes out from my mouth; it shall not return to me empty.

(ISAIAH 55:10–11A, ESV)

God rules nature. While humans might be able to predict the weather, we have yet to create weather out of nothing—much less to coordinate a series of global processes that effectively sustain the entire planet. The balance and intricacy of it point straight to our Creator God in a magnificent display of both His sovereignty and His providence. He rules it because He created it.

Jesus once displayed His sovereign rule over weather during a violent squall while in a boat on the Sea of Galilee. He rebuked the wind and sea, and by His word, all became calm. Even his followers (which included professional fishermen) were amazed: "Who is this? Even the wind and the waves obey Him!"

God is not only sovereign over weather, He also provides through its many systems. His sustenance of us in this most basic way for survival is a picture of how He provides for us in a myriad of ways—including His Word. God has given us *everything* we need for both life and godliness.

Discussion

How do you see the sovereignty and providence of God displayed through weather?

How do you see His sovereign care and provision in your own life?

For Further Reading

Psalm 89:8–9, Jeremiah 14:22, Jeremiah 10:12–13, 2 Peter 1:3

#

PSALM 148

Praise the Lord!
Praise the Lord from the heavens;
Praise Him in the heights!
Praise Him, all His angels;
Praise Him, all His hosts!

Praise Him, sun and moon,
Praise Him, all you shining stars!
Praise Him, you highest heavens,
And you waters above the heavens!

Let them praise the name of the Lord!
For He commanded and they were created.
And He established them forever and ever;
He gave a decree, and it shall not pass away.

Praise the Lord from the earth,
You great sea creatures and all deeps,
Fire and hail, snow and mist,
Stormy wind fulfilling His Word!

(Psalm 148:1–8, ESV)

\#

IT IS WELL WITH MY SOUL
AUTHOR: HORATIO SPAFFORD

Saved alone. What shall I do?

The wife of Horatio Spafford sent him a telegram with these words following a shipwreck. All four of his daughters drowned. Anna was found unconscious, floating on debris.

His life had echoes of Job. Just two years earlier, his son died of scarlet fever and the Great Chicago Fire reduced his many real estate properties to ashes.

He was supposed to be on that ship with his family. They had planned a vacation to England and were to sail on the steamship *Ville du Havre*. But at the last minute, he had to attend to business, so Horatio put his family onboard and delayed his own departure.

The *Ville du Havre* collided with an iron clipper. In the wake of tragedy, Anna said, "God gave me four daughters. Now they have been taken from me. Someday I will understand why."

Upon receiving the telegram, Horatio immediately set off to bring his wife home. On the way, the sea captain alerted Horatio when they passed over the spot where the ship sank.

Horatio later gave an account of it in a letter to Anna's half sister: "On Thursday last we passed over the spot where she went down, in mid-ocean, the waters three miles deep. But I do not think of our dear ones there. They are safe, folded, the dear lambs."

And it was out of this mixture of grief and faith that Horatio penned the words: "When peace like a river attendeth my way, when sorrows like sea billows roll; whatever my lot Thou hast taught me say, it is well, it is well with my soul...."

Song

When peace, like a river, attendeth my way,
When sorrows like sea billows roll;
Whatever my lot, Thou hast taught me to say,
It is well, it is well with my soul.

Though Satan should buffet, though trials should come,
Let this blest assurance control,
That Christ hath regarded my helpless estate,
And hath shed His own blood for my soul.

My sin, oh the bliss of this glorious thought!
My sin, not in part but the whole,
Is nailed to His cross, and I bear it no more,
Praise the Lord, praise the Lord, O my soul!

For me, be it Christ, be it Christ hence to live:
If Jordan above me shall roll,
No pain shall be mine, for in death as in life
Thou wilt whisper Thy peace to my soul.

And Lord haste the day, when the faith shall be sight,
The clouds be rolled back as a scroll;
The trump shall resound, and the Lord shall descend
Even so, it is well with my soul.

For Further Reading

Psalm 42:5–8

#

SETTING AN ANCHOR

A captain and his crew sail into the lee of an island. After a long day on the water, all are tired and hungry, but first they must set the anchor. They make quick work of it. Overnight, the crash of waves jolts the captain awake. Bolting to the deck, his fears are realized—the boat is drifting toward shore. This time he properly resets the anchor.

Anchoring involves way more than "dropping" the anchor. It requires the sharp focus of mind and senses; there is no rushing the process.

Using charts or prior knowledge, the captain must predetermine the right anchorage. Is it protected from wind? What type of bottom? The best sea bottom allows the anchor to penetrate; however, rock, vegetation, loose sand, and soft mud all present their challenges. In rock, the anchor wedges precariously into a crevice. In vegetation, it often pulls grass up by its roots. In loose sand or very soft mud, it simply has nothing to grab.

Approaching the anchorage slowly, a wise captain will consider other boats and underwater conditions (e.g., shoals). He will position the boat into the wind and lower the anchor. Once it reaches the bottom, he lets out the amount of rode necessary to prevent dragging or swinging into neighboring boats—called scope—reverses to encourage the anchor to bite, and then makes the line fast thereby setting the anchor. Next he checks and checks again that the anchor has held secure. In threatening conditions, the captain might order an anchor watch in which a crewmember monitors the boat's position via GPS or compass bearings to objects on land.

If the anchor is not properly set, the boat is sure to drift at the mercy of wind and current. A well-set anchor in a good anchorage should hold, even in a storm.

Did You Know?

The Isles of Shoals off the coast of New Hampshire and Maine is a challenging anchorage and not only for its shoals. Known as the "anchor graveyard," its seabed is littered with lost anchors—anchors lodged into rock or entangled with other anchors.

Key Scripture

We have this as a sure and steadfast anchor of the soul, a hope that enters into the inner place behind the curtain, where Jesus has gone as a forerunner on our behalf, having become a high priest forever.

(HEBREWS 6:19–20A, ESV)

We must pay the most careful attention, therefore, to what we have heard, so that we do not drift away.

(HEBREWS 2:1, NIV)

Choosing the right anchor in life is critical. The wrong anchor is an unsafe idol that cannot save. In fact, we will simply drift at the behest of our circumstances. But scripture teaches that our hope in Jesus is a secure anchor, and this hope is not the wisp of a wish. It is a confidence that rests squarely on Jesus, who Is our hope and who intercedes for us before the throne of God.

If Christ is the anchor, then what is the sea soil? In His parable of the sower, Jesus drew parallels between the soul and soil, Word and seed. He described four types of soil—good, thorny, rocky, and hard. When the seed of the Word landed on good soil, the person was able to both hear and understand the Word—it took root and flourished. So it is when our anchor deeply penetrates our lives.

It is not enough to declare offhand that Christ is our anchor—like simply dropping an anchor over the side. Rather, we seek to understand Jesus as revealed in His Word which builds trust. We stay alert, preparing for storms. Then we can rest in our Anchor, even in a storm, because He is our hope and we know Him.

Life's toughest storms prove the strength of our anchors. Money, prestige, reputation, and even loved ones are false anchors, but Christ remains a sure and steadfast anchor for the soul.

Discussion

Who or what is your anchor?

How would you describe the "sea soil" of your soul?

For Further Reading

Hebrews 4:14–16, Matthew 13:18–23, James 1:5–8, Proverbs 10:25, Ephesians 3:17–19

\#

DEAD CALM

Wind is to us what money is to life on shore. (Sterling Hayden) Sailors depend on wind, but what if there is no wind at all? To describe a typical scene: The sails flap, effectively bringing the vessel to a stop—our very own braking system. The wind indicator at the top of the mast spins. The water goes flat. The sky is cloudless, so the sun is hot and the air is still. And to top it all off, the flies begin to bite.

Vast areas in the ocean are known for these calms. Known as the horse latitudes, or doldrums, this area of high pressure sits at thirty degrees north and south of the equator. The advent of engines and upwind sailing has changed our experience of the "horse latitudes" from that of previous centuries. Dead calm, for them, meant bobbing along until the weather changed. Often the captain had problems with managing crew behavior and morale during this time. They were truly at the mercy of the wind.

Today, we either patiently wait for wind or impatiently turn on that engine.

Did You Know?

In the past centuries, sea captains relied on the trade winds to carry them from Europe down to the West Indies. If they got caught in that area of high pressure, legend has it they would throw horses overboard to both lighten the load and preserve drinking water, thus, the horse latitudes.

Key Scripture

Be still and know that I am God.

(PSALM 46:10A, ESV)

Much analogy has been made out of the "storms" of life, but what about those times when our lives sail straight into a dead calm? All appears sunny on the outside, with no reason to complain, and yet inside we are shriveling. Perhaps we feel aimless, without purpose, apathetic, complacent, discontent, or bored.

We are waiting.

I read about one sailor going through the horse latitudes. He was grateful for the gentle wind that moved them along—albeit slowly—and he saw the dolphins playing in the wake of the ship. The man was *grateful* and *saw* in the middle of the calm.

Sometimes our busy lives are so choked with distractions that God gives us our own horse latitudes. What appears to be without purpose might have a world of purpose behind it. Am I grateful in the desert calm? Do I see the dolphins? More than that, am I trusting God and listening to Him?

Be still and know that I am God. The word translated "be still" is actually pretty strong—more like "shut up and listen!" He is both God in the storm *and* God in the calm. The prophet Elijah waited alone in a cave for a word from the Lord. God did not answer Elijah through the great and strong wind (nor the earthquake, nor the fire), rather, through a still, small voice.

Oh, that we would not turn on our figurative engines and drown out the voice of God!

Discussion

Have you ever experienced a spiritual dead calm?

How do you build time in your day to listen to God?

Are there places or practices that help you listen to God's voice?

For Further Reading

1 Kings 19:11–12, Psalm 27:13–14

#

SEA STORY FROM MATTHEW: WALKING ON WATER

Immediately He made the disciples get into the boat and go before Him to the other side, while He dismissed the crowds. And after He had dismissed the crowds, He went up on the mountain by Himself to pray.

When evening came, He was there alone, but the boat by this time was a long way from the land, beaten by the waves, for the wind was against them.

And in the fourth watch of the night He came to them, walking on the sea. But when the disciples saw Him walking on the sea, they were terrified, and said, "It is a ghost!" and they cried out in fear.

But immediately Jesus spoke to them, saying, "Take heart; it is I. Do not be afraid."

And Peter answered Him, "Lord, if it is you, command me to come to you on the water."

He said, "Come."

So Peter got out of the boat and walked on the water and came to Jesus. But when he saw the wind, he was afraid, and beginning to sink he cried out, "Lord, save me."

Jesus immediately reached out His hand and took hold of him, saying to him, "O you of little faith, why did you doubt?"

And when they got into the boat, the wind ceased. And those in the boat worshiped Him, saying, "Truly you are the Son of God." (Matthew 14:22–33, ESV)

#

WAVES

To the novice any vertical motion in the water is referred to as waves; however, a good sailor knows the difference in the various types of waves and the distinctive root cause.

Swells are most often only found at sea. Swells are the gentle rolling of the ocean. They probably originated days and thousands of miles away, so the ocean sailor must understand the reason for larger than normal swells. It may be an approaching large system with strong winds or a tropical storm. If the swells are big and far apart, the ride can be relatively pleasant. Steep swells that are large and close together can be challenging.

Waves are generated by winds. Waves generally ride on top of swells. Waves exist on all bodies of water, not just the ocean. The size of waves depends on the strength and duration of the wind and the size of the body of water. The longer the winds have been blowing across a larger body of water, the higher the waves. This is called fetch. If you go out sailing on a large body of water and the wind has been blowing strong for several days, you can expect that the fetch will have produced higher waves. Conversely, a squall that moves over a flat body of water will not be present long enough to generate much in the way of waves, so after the squall passes, the water will flatten again.

It is also useful to know which direction the waves are coming relative to the direction you will be sailing; perpendicular waves taken on the beam will make for a rougher ride and probably more seasick crew.

Finally, just as waves ride on top of swells, there are ripples, called zephyrs or "cat's-paws" that ride on top of waves. Zephyrs indicate small variations in wind conditions such as gusts. Racers, in particular, watch for and respond to ripples moving across the water to take advantage of approaching gusts.

Key Scripture

But let him ask with faith... for the one who doubts is like a wave of the sea that is driven and tossed by the wind.

(JAMES 1:6, ESV)

Faith and doubts. Doubt is an unstable belief. A thought enters in—do I *really* believe and trust this? When the serpent suggested to Eve that she shouldn't trust the goodness of God, he planted a doubt that threw off her faith in the very One who gave her life. Even today, we face figurative serpents assaulting our beliefs. A personal belief system that relies solely on traditions, empty rituals, and head knowledge will come crashing down, but trusting in a God we *know* will anchor our faith.

When Jesus walked on water, impervious to the waves and wind, it was a picture of His rule over all creation, for what person can walk with confidence on what is not designed to be walked on, except for the One who created it? Enter Peter who stepped into the lesson of a spiritual principle. When he had his eyes on Jesus, he too walked securely on water. But the moment Peter looked at his surroundings, he began to sink. Jesus rescued Peter with these words: "O you of little faith, why did you doubt?" Then

Jesus further showed His power over wind and wave by speaking them into stillness.

I can almost hear Jesus asking, "Do you know Whom you have believed?"

Spiritual double-mindedness is to be tossed about in the no-man's-land of oscillating faith and disbelief—a dangerous place to be. Jesus is not calling us to walk on literal water, defying the laws of physics that He Himself instituted. He's calling us to what it represents—in unstable circumstances, look at Me, believe Me, and *trust* Me! Do not take on the properties of a wave driven by wind.

Discussion

What are particular ideas or situations that can cause you to question your faith?

For Further Reading

James 1:5–8, Psalm 89:8–9, Ephesians 4:14–15, Hebrews 12:1–2, 2 Timothy 1:12

#

TIDES

For most of human history, tides have been a mystery. Even today, much about tides remains unknown.

The gravitational pull of the sun and moon as the earth rotates is a primary cause of tide cycle. The moon is the strongest force. The moon's gravity pulls the ocean toward it, causing a high tide on the side of the earth toward the moon and a high tide on the side away from the moon with two low tides on either side. Full moon and new moon produce the strongest pull and, therefore, the greatest tidal ranges. Other factors impacting tidal range include the characteristics of land mass—narrow and deep versus wide and shallow—winds, atmospheric pressure, and more.

Most areas of the world experience two high tides and two low tides per day, although some experience only one tide cycle. Tide predictions apply historical trends to current data rather than applying a formula that considers all the several hundred factors involved.

Sailors need to know two primary things:

1. How much will the water rise and fall at a particular time of day? This is necessary information for knowing the right time to cross a reef, to pass under a bridge, and the amount of rode to let out at anchor.

2. What are the tidal currents? When tides rise and fall, there is an associated current as water flows from one location to another. Knowing the speed and direction of this current at a certain time can allow you to get somewhere faster (if the current is flowing with you) or get there at all (if the current is flowing against you or pushing you off course). A sailboat motoring out against the incoming tidal flow will have difficulty transiting an inlet from the bay to ocean.

A competent sailor knows his tide tables and depends on certain things to happen at the predicted time.

Key Scripture

He is the radiance of the glory of God and the exact imprint of his nature, and he upholds the universe by the word of his power.

(HEBREWS 1:3A, ESV)

We sometimes view God as the Creator of the universe who set everything in motion and then let whatever happens happen. This is particularly true when challenges come into our life that we cannot understand—such as death, cruelty, and sickness, just to name a few.

However, scripture reveals a God who is involved in the miniscule details of everything and everywhere. Colossians 1:16–17 (ESV) says that *all things are created through him and for him, and in Him all things hold together.* The Gospels tell us that every day God makes sure the birds are fed, the flowers are well-dressed, and even the hairs on our heads are numbered.* No detail is too insignificant to escape God's attention and care.

Theologians call this God's *providence*. The providence of God is the basis for predictability in this world. The sun will come up in the morning at a predictable time. Seeds will grow into the same species. Wood will burn for fire, and, yes, the tides will ebb and flow on schedule. Even a minor change in the tilt of the earth on its axis or its distance from the sun would be disastrous. If the moon were closer, the tides would sweep in and flood the land. As designed, tides provide tremendous value by moving vast amounts of seawater to replenish various areas and transfer heat; all this results in a more stable climate.

In short, God holds all things in perfect order by His providence.

Discussion

Are there times in your life when it is hard to believe that God is in control?

What are ways you have seen the providence of God working in the details of your life?

For Further Reading

Psalm 135:6–7, *Matthew 6:26–34, 10:29–31, Luke 12:24–29

#

PSALM 147

Praise the LORD!
For it is good to sing praises to our God;
for it is pleasant, and a song of praise is fitting.

The LORD builds up Jerusalem;
He gathers the outcasts of Israel.
He heals the brokenhearted and binds up their wounds.
He determines the number of the stars;
He gives to all of them their names.
Great is our Lord, and abundant in power;
His understanding is beyond measure...

He covers the heavens with clouds;
He prepares rain for the earth;
He makes grass grow on the hills.
He gives to the beasts their food,
and to the young ravens that cry...

He strengthens the bars of your gates;
He blesses your children within you.
He makes peace in your borders;

He fills you with the finest of the wheat.
He sends out his command to the earth;
His word runs swiftly.
He gives snow like wool;
He scatters frost like ashes.
He hurls down his crystals of ice like crumbs;
who can stand before his cold?

He sends out his word, and melts them;
He makes his wind blow and the waters flow.
He declares his word to Jacob,
His statutes and rules to Israel...

Praise the LORD!

(Psalm 147:1–5, 8–9, 13–19, 20b, ESV)

#

AMAZING GRACE
AUTHOR: JOHN NEWTON

JOHN NEWTON *CLERK* ONCE AN INFIDEL AND LIBERTINE A SERVANT OF SLAVES IN AFRICA WAS BY THE RICH MERCY OF OUR **LORD** AND **SAVIOUR JESUS CHRIST**, PRESERVED, RESTORED, PARDONED, AND APPOINTED TO PREACH THE FAITH HE HAD LONG LABOURED TO DESTROY.

The words above are inscribed on John Newton's tombstone, writer of arguably the most famous hymn of all time—*Amazing Grace*. Like his self-epitaph, the hymn was Newton's testimony.

John was a British eighteenth-century slave trader who digressed so far into vile living that even his slave-trading father rejected him for a season. After a stint in jail, Newton returned to the sea and his trade but was so despised by the crew that they abandoned him in West Africa. There, Princess Peye—a native of Sierra Leone—made him her slave and abused the former slave trader.

At his prolonged absence, John's father sent a sea captain to search for his son. He finally found John in early 1748 and rescued him from the princess. On their return journey, the ship sailed into a violent storm off the coast of Ireland. As the ship began to fill with water, John cried out to God. Miraculously, he survived the shipwreck. That storm at sea became his turning point. John began reading the Bible and put his faith in Jesus Christ on March 10, 1748.

John continued in the slave trade but eventually retired to become a minister—writing hymns and serving his congregation. Thirty-eight years after retiring from the sea, Newton joined forces with the famous abolitionist, William Wilberforce, and spoke these words: "I hope it will always be a subject of humiliating reflection to me that I was once an active instrument in a business at which my heart now shudders."

That heart transformation reflected the far deeper transformation God had worked within John.

Song

Amazing Grace, how sweet the sound,
That saved a wretch like me.
I once was lost but now I'm found,
Was blind, but now I see.

'Twas Grace that taught,
my heart to fear.
And grace, my fears relieved.
How precious did that grace appear,
the hour I first believed.

Through many dangers, toils and snares,
I have already come.
'tis grace that brought me safe thus far,
and grace will lead us home.

The Lord has promised good to me,
His word my hope secures.
He will my shield and portion be,
as long as life endures.

Yes, when this flesh and heart shall fail,
And mortal life shall cease;
I shall possess, within the veil,
A life of joy and peace.

The earth shall soon dissolve like snow,
The sun forbear to shine;
But God, who call'd me here below,
Will be forever mine.

For Further Reading

Ephesians 2:1–9, Galatians 5:1

#

THE IMPORTANCE OF A NAME

E verything on a sailboat has a name. This practice dates back centuries and is necessary to properly and safely operate a vessel. When the officer speaks (or yells) an order, the crew must know exactly what to do. Imagine if the officer commanded "tighten that rope or sail to the left!"

Confusion would ensue. The sailor would wonder, "Which rope? My left or your left?"

Therefore, every line and function has a specific name. What is a mere rope to a non-sailor could be the jib sheet, main halyard, outhaul, reefing line, and the list goes on.

Port, starboard, bow, stern, forward, aft, and abeam all define a direction not relative to the sailor (and where he or she is standing) but relative to the ship itself.

The points of sail—close hauled, close reach, beam reach, broad reach, and running all—describe the location of the wind relative to the boat.

The many names are a lot to learn but oh so important. Let's say an unexpected storm pops up or an enemy vessel appears on the horizon; the captain does not have time to define every word and action to his crew.

So even today if the captain orders "tack to starboard and stay close hauled," the crew knows exactly what he means and what to do.

Aye Aye, Captain! (Yes, even so, Captain!)

The name itself is the definition.

Key Scripture

Hallowed be Your name.

(MATTHEW 6:9c, ESV)

In the ancient world, a personal name had great significance—defining a person's character or identity. Abraham meant *father of a multitude.* Isaac meant *laughter.* Jacob meant *he cheats.*

The same is true for God's name. Why is God's name to be hallowed or revered? Because His Name—above all other names—defines His very essence!

We could fill pages with the many names of God, but there is one name in particular that God used as His personal name: Yahweh or *to be.* God first revealed this name to Moses. In our Bibles, Yahweh is translated LORD (note the uppercase). Jews consider this personal name of God too sacred to speak, so they abbreviate it to YHWH.

Yahweh sounds like I AM in Hebrew. And Yahweh *is* the I AM—the self-existent, eternal, sovereign Lord of all that is. Jesus boldly claimed the divine name for himself: "Truly, truly, I say to you, before Abraham was, I AM" (John 8:58).

The name I AM consumes all else. For example, we might look at a sunset and call it beautiful; however, God is beauty itself. He is the I AM. The sunset would not be beautiful apart from its reflection of God who is the source of all beauty.

God deliberately uses His many names to teach us who He is so we can know Him.

Discussion

Can you think of other names of God?

What is a definition of that name?

What do those names teach us about who God is?

For Further Reading

Exodus 3:13–15, Genesis 32:24–30, John 8:53–58, Philippians 2:5–11

#

Running Aground

A great ship asks for deep waters.

(Romanian Proverb)

A competent helmsman and navigator work together to monitor depths under the keel using nautical charts and objects on land as a reference. Even so, most sailors will run aground multiple times. As the saying goes, *if you haven't run aground, you haven't been around.* The hope is that the ground is forgiving, like the mud of the Chesapeake rather than the rocks off the coast of Maine. In either case, it is important to be prepared and alert and to know what to do. From the first thud, the key is to stop forward progress. Trying to force your way over a shoal will only dig you in deeper.

It is entirely possible that despite all efforts, the boat is hopelessly stuck. Perhaps you have a crew of people that will help to work the keel off by moving furthest from the point of impact to either redistribute ballast or (in the case of a soft bottom) to rock the boat loose. Perhaps another boat will offer to provide a tow.

Or perhaps it is simply a matter of time—waiting for the tide to rise.

Key Scripture

Repent therefore, and turn again, that your sins may be blotted out, that times of refreshing may come from the presence of the Lord.

(ACTS 3:19–20A, ESV)

Every Christian runs aground, even on a daily basis. Some area of sin that so easily entangles can strike at any time. The key is to confess our sins and repent. Repent means to turn around and go the other way. Becoming a Christian does not mean that we cease sinning, but rather we get up from a fall going in the right direction. Becoming more like Christ (called sanctification) is not our work but God's work, and He will accomplish what He promises. When we sin, we must not lose heart but trust God to continue to change our heart. Faith leads to obedience.

Many times, we find ourselves completely stuck as a consequence of sin. We want to repent, but we are in such a fix, it takes a while to come through on the other side. Sometimes God gives us people to rally around us, hold us accountable, and actively help us out of our messes.

And sometimes we have to wait on Him.

Another way we can remain stuck in the mire of running spiritually aground is to dwell on our past failure. Does guilt haunt us even after we confess our sin? Do we believe in His promise to forgive?

Discussion

Can you think of a time when you ran spiritually aground?

How has God provided the strength and tools to overcome sin?

Was there a time when others helped you through?

Describe a time when you waited on God.

For Further Reading

Isaiah 30:15a, Hebrews 12:1–3, 1 John 1:9, Philippians1:6, Mark 9:23–24

#

SHORTCUTS AND GRACE

A sailing magazine features a popular section where sailors tell their tales of often harrowing experiences on the water—popular because we all like a dramatic story and popular, too, because we wonder what we would do in the same situation. In each issue, the author shares the experience and then includes two bullet point lists: first, what we did right and, second, what we did wrong.

As sailors, we don't need to read articles to know that we've all been there, having swapped many of our own stories. Sometimes these stories are born out of circumstances beyond our control, many times from human error.

It could be as simple as a line handler jumping for a finger pier while docking on a gusty day; down she goes between the boat and dock into cold April waters. In her impatience, she misjudged.

Or perhaps a sailor is weary after a long, happy day on the water, and rather than lowering his mast, he decides to drive his trailered boat the short distance home—mast raised and all. Never mind the power lines on the way; surely his daysailer would clear. He was wrong.

(Yes, these are true stories we have heard around a table!)

Maybe a boat is sailing *on a schedule* down the bay from Annapolis to Solomons Island in a prevailing south wind. The captain knows that he is low on diesel—fuel is his backup in the event of wind on the nose or no wind at all. The fuel dock is busy. With time pressing on him, he sets off without fueling up or taking along extra jerry cans of diesel. This boat is not prepared for the journey.

When we listen to these stories of shortcuts, if we are honest, we can probably relate. We inwardly shake our heads in a mixture of judgment and understanding and say to ourselves, "But for the grace of God."

Key Scripture

For by grace you have been saved through faith. And this is not your own doing; it is the gift of God, not a result of works, so that no one may boast.

(EPHESIANS 2:8–9, ESV)

Justice. Mercy. Grace. To better understand the rich meaning of these three simple words, let's apply them to the illustration of the captain heading down the bay low on fuel with the wind on his nose.

Justice: Tacking down the bay in a south wind, the captain is forced to motor. He runs out of fuel on the way and misses his deadline. He gets what he deserves—that is justice.

Mercy: Tacking down the bay in a south wind, the captain is forced to motor. He worries the whole way, but he does not run out of fuel and arrives on time. He does not get what he deserves—that is mercy.

Grace: Let's up the ante and say the captain has risked this before. In his impatience and procrastination, he habitually sets out unprepared against a south wind, and here he goes again. Miraculously, the prevailing south wind shifts to twenty knots on his beam. The unprepared captain sails down the bay in record time. That wind shift is a gift. Not only did he not get what he deserved (mercy), but he received a gift he did absolutely nothing to earn. That is grace.

In our key scripture above, the Greek word for grace is *Charis*. *Charis* could also be translated "gift" because grace means gift.

Take a look at the key scripture again. We do not earn our salvation any more than that captain earned the beautiful gift of wind on his beam. Salvation is God's gift of grace to us!

Discussion

Have you ever experienced God's grace?

Do you sometimes feel that you have to earn His favor by being good or doing good deeds?

For Further Reading

Ephesians 2:4–10; Psalm 103:1–14

#

TEACH THEM TO YEARN

If you want to build a ship, don't drum up the men to gather wood and give orders. Instead teach them to yearn for the vast and endless sea.

ANTOINE DE SAINT-EXUPÉRY

O nce a person catches the sailing bug, he is prone to make a lot of decisions that don't appear to make sense. He is so in love with sailing that he makes it a priority and spends money that he will likely never get back. This was certainly true for us.

We saw a glimpse of this same sailing bug come to life in a promising young man. We had taken a group of younger teen boys out for a sail through a local outreach program. This program was designed to give kids experiences they would not otherwise have.

When we first met the boys, they were pretty timid as we helped them from dock to boat. None of them had ever been on a boat, most were not swimmers (yes, they were wearing PFDs!), and many had never crossed the nearby Chesapeake Bay Bridge or even laid eyes on the bay though they lived the next county over. They were a little scared and a lot nervous as we headed out of Annapolis Harbor.

But it was a perfect day for sailing! Soon we had each boy at the helm, teaching them what to do and letting them feel the wind in their hands. It gave us joy to watch their fear give way to pure delight.

Toward the end of our sail, I settled next to the boy who was the most frightened at the beginning. With relaxed, happy eyes and a huge grin, he turned to me and said, "When I grow up, I'm going to get a boat and sail this ocean!"

We saw it firsthand—Antoine's de Saint-Exupéry's quote—and it took only a few short hours, but he was already yearning for the vast and endless sea of the Chesapeake Bay.

Key Scripture

No one can come to me unless the Father who sent me draws him.

(JOHN 6:44, ESV)

Our nature is to live our Christian life as a religion, attempting to reach God by doing good works. However, this is impossible. Scripture teaches that "by works of the law no human being will be justified in His sight." Perhaps we know that we are saved by grace alone but think that we have to live the rest of our Christian life doing good works out of a determined sense of duty—*God saved me, but it's up to me now!* This fallacy will only set us on an endless, joyless treadmill of performance.

The Pharisees and scribes of Jesus's time were more concerned about rules, traditions, and external appearances than their inner hearts before God. Jesus called them white-washed tombs, saying, "This people honors me with their lips, but their heart is far from me; in vain do they worship me, teaching as doctrines the commandments of men."* Theirs was the sterile obedience to religious practice, not a yearning for God Himself.

When one of those scribes asked, "What is the great commandment?", Jesus pulled the truth out of that scribe: love the

68

Lord your God with all your heart, mind, soul, and strength; further, all the law hangs off of this love.

Love comes first, and obedience is born out of that love, not the other way around. My inner heart before God always precedes any external behavior.

Jesus teaches us to yearn for Him, and we are only able to do that because He first loved us.

Discussion

Do you yearn for God out of love for who He is and a response of gratitude?

Do you yearn for the gift or the Giver?

Do you ever strive for God out of duty or feel you have to perform for Him?

For Further Reading

Romans 3:20–23, Galatians 3:2–3, *Matthew 15:6–9, 1 John 4:15–19, John 14:23

#

PSALM 139

If I rise on the wings of the dawn,
if I settle on the far side of the sea,
even there your hand will guide me,
your right hand will hold me fast.

(Psalm 139:9–10)

#

FEATURED SEA STORY: SHIPWRECKED!

...three times I was shipwrecked; a night and a day I was adrift at sea, on frequent journeys, in danger from rivers, danger from robbers, danger from my own people, danger from Gentiles, danger in the city, danger in the wilderness, danger at sea....

(THE APOSTLE PAUL IN HIS SECOND LETTER TO
THE CHURCH OF CORINTH, ESV)

The book of Acts ends in the climax of Paul's voyage as a prisoner from Caesarea to Rome to stand before Caesar. Luke's eyewitness account of the journey spans two chapters (Acts 27–28) and is filled with nautical terms.

The first leg of their 2000-mile voyage was on a smaller trading vessel, the Adramyttium, which sailed to ports along the coast: from Caesarea to Sidon to Myra in modern-day Turkey.

And putting out to sea from there we sailed under the lee of Cyprus, because the winds were against us.

(27:4, ESV)

Had the wind been in their favor, it would have been faster to sail windward of Cyprus, but the predominant westerly wind made it impossible to make progress. Instead, they sailed under the lee or on the protected side of Cyprus away from the wind.

Windward: the side facing the wind
Leeward: the side away from the wind
Westerly: wind is named by the direction from which it comes

The prisoners disembarked at Myra and boarded a large grain freighter bound for Rome. The largest grain freighters of the time were 180 ft with a 50 ft beam. We do not know the exact size of Paul's freighter, but we do know it was no small vessel; it carried wheat and 276 passengers and crew. The port of Myra was a hub for these large freighters to move between Alexandria and Rome. Here began the second leg of their journey.

The freighter of prisoners and wheat hugged the coast, fighting the wind. Off Cnidus, they were forced once more to turn and sail under the lee of Crete. Finally, rounding the island, they stopped in the port of Fair Havens south of Crete.

...much time had passed, and the voyage was now dangerous, because even the Fast was already over....

(27:9, ESV)

The Fast was the Day of Atonement (i.e., Yom Kippur) which takes place in October. We have hurricane season on our side of the Atlantic between June and November; the Mediterranean's storm season falls between September and January and includes weather events called the euroquilos. These strong east-northeast winds can be cyclonic and primarily occur to the west of Crete—at the same time of year and in the same direction the prison ship was headed.

Paul's Unheeded Warning in Fair Havens

Sirs, I perceive that the voyage will be with injury and much loss, not only of the cargo and the ship, but also of our lives.

(27:10, ESV)

The owner of the ship did not want to winter in Fair Havens as the port was very much exposed to the elements. It would endanger his assets of both ship and cargo. So they departed and attempted to reach the port of Phoenix—a natural harbor protected from storm winds (Luke describes it as facing both southwest and northwest) with sufficient depth for the large freighter.

Now when the south wind blew gently... they weighed anchor and sailed along Crete, close to the shore. But soon a tempestuous wind, called the northeaster, struck down from the land. And when the ship was caught and could not face the wind, we gave way to it and were driven along.

(27:13–15, ESV)

Weigh anchor: to take up the anchor

Freed of the seabed, a gentle south wind would have been ideal to make their desired port. It was a gamble that did not pay off. The violent windstorm came over the island from the northeast and took control of the ship. They were driven toward the small island of Cauda (modern-day Gavdos) which is southwest of Crete. Leeward of Cauda, they hoisted the lifeboat up to the deck and undergirded the ship. Luke indicated this was no easy task.

Undergird: also called frapping; to strengthen an ancient ship in violent storms by passing ropes underneath its hull

Then, fearing that they would run aground on the Syrtis, they lowered the gear, and thus they were driven along.

(27:17, ESV)

The Syrtis were deadly shallows off the coast of North Africa. Strabo, a geographer who traveled the Roman Empire extensively and died ca. 24 AD, wrote: "the difficulty with both the Greater and the Lesser Syrtes is that in many places the water is shallow, and at the rise and fall of the tides ships sometimes fall into the shallows and settle there, and it is rare for them to be saved" (Strabo's Geography, 17.3.20).

The topography, weather, and tides worked against these ancient mariners. Two long fingers of sandbars extend far out into the sea, entrapping large ships amid underwater sand dunes. The strong three-knot clockwise current when flooding and counterclockwise turn when ebbing result in a constant reversing of the sea as it moves in and out. Mariners avoided the Syrtis at all costs.

In the case of Paul's Alexandrian freighter, the weight of all those people and cargo put them still further at risk. The ship was likely taking on water. First, they lowered the gear—either the sails or sea anchor or both— and then jettisoned the cargo (all that potential profit of wheat lost after all) and finally, the ship's tackle.

Paul's Encouragement in the Storm

Men, you should have listened to me and not have set sail from Crete and incurred this injury and loss. Yet now I urge you to take heart, for there will be no loss of life among you, but only of the ship. For this very night there stood before me an angel of the God to whom I belong and whom I worship, and he said, 'Do not be afraid, Paul; you must stand before Caesar. And behold, God has granted you all those who sail with you.' So take heart, men, for I have faith in God that it will be exactly as I have been told. But we must run aground on some island.

(27:21–26, ESV)

The ship floundered in the Mediterranean for two weeks. Around midnight on the fourteenth night, the sailors sensed land so they took a sounding. Twenty fathoms. A little farther—another sounding. Fifteen fathoms. Fearing wreckage on rocks, they let out four anchors off the stern of the ship.

Sounding: to measure depth of water using a line with a plummet or lead weight at the end
Fathom: measurement of water depth equal to six feet

Paul's Heeded Warning at Midnight

Paul said to the centurion and the soldiers, "Unless these men stay in the ship, you cannot be saved." Then the soldiers cut away the ropes of the ship's boat and let it go.

(27:31–32, ESV)

Between midnight and dawn, drama unfolded. The sailors unsuccessfully tried to abandon the ship under a ruse of letting out bow anchors. Paul put a stop to it. At dawn, all ate, and then they lightened the ship by throwing out the remaining wheat.

Breaking Bread

"Today is the fourteenth day that you have continued in suspense and without food, having taken nothing. Therefore I urge you to take some food. For it will give you strength, for not a hair is to perish from the head of any of you." And when he had said these things, he took bread, and giving thanks to God in the presence of all he broke it and began to eat. Then they all were encouraged and ate some food themselves.

(27:33–36, ESV)

By light of day, none of the seasoned sailors recognized the land. They cast off the four anchors they had let out overnight and loosened the ropes they had used to secure the rudders all the way back in Cauda fourteen days before. Then they hoisted the foresail and made for the beach.

Shipwreck

The soldiers plan was to kill the prisoners, lest any should swim away and escape. But the centurion, wishing to save Paul, kept them from carrying out their plan... And so it was that all were brought safely to land.

(27:42–44, ESV)

The ship ran aground at the place between the two seas. The bow stuck, immovable, and the stern broke up in the violent surf. The ship was falling apart. All swam for shore or used planks or pieces of ship, and all 276 survived the shipwreck.

Paul on Malta

Paul visited him and prayed, and putting his hands on him healed him. And when this had taken place, the rest of the people on the island who had diseases also came and were cured. They also honored us greatly, and when we were about to sail, they put on board whatever we needed.

(28:8–10, ESV)

They were on the small island of Malta, south of Sicily, and wintered there until storm season was over. Three months later, the prisoners boarded a new Egyptian grain ship from Malta to Syracuse in Sicily, to Rhegium on the tip of Italy's boot, to Puteoli in the Gulf of Naples. From there Paul traveled by land to Rome.

#

THE SHORTEST DISTANCE

"You can't change the wind, but you can adjust your sails."

Sailing is not for the impatient... or the rushed. It is only logical that when trying to get from Point A to Point B, one would choose the shortest distance. But what is true on terra firma is not necessarily true in a sailboat on water.

In sailing, points of sail define the direction of wind relative to the boat (see figure below). Close hauled is the point of sail closest to the wind. Any closer than that and the boat stalls or goes into irons; this is true for wind coming from anywhere within forty-five degrees off the bow of the boat.

If the desired destination is in the same direction as the wind, one simply cannot sail the shortest distance between two points. Instead, the sailor may choose to sail close hauled using a technique known as tacking (bringing the bow across the wind and adjusting the sails accordingly) to make consistent progress to windward. Or perhaps the wind mandates a change in destination.

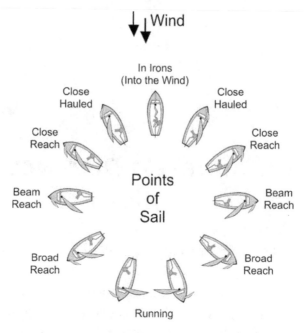

Wind

In Irons
(Into the Wind)

Close
Hauled

Close
Hauled

Close
Reach

Close
Reach

Points
of
Sail

Beam
Reach

Beam
Reach

Broad
Reach

Broad
Reach

Running

Source: American Sailing Association

Key Scripture

All the paths of the Lord are steadfast love and faithfulness, for those who keep His covenant and testimonies.

(PSALM 25:10, ESV)

A path implies a destination. How many times have we been on a straight path that takes a wild turn? We might point in what appears to be the shortest distance and protest, "But I am supposed to go there!" We might even pray, "Lord, what are you doing?" or "Where are you taking me?" or maybe simply "Why, God?!"

In Psalm 25, David seems to be on a confusing path. He clearly doesn't know what God is doing, yet he doesn't say *some* or even *most* paths of the Lord are loving and faithful. No, he says *all* paths.

What if he had declared his rights as king and followed only the path of his own reasoning—the shortest distance? After all, a leader needs to lead, take control, and decide. David might have stalled out in irons, unable to make forward progress. Worse still, he might have put himself and his entire kingdom in jeopardy. Perhaps God's path was strengthening David's own character as David leaned further on Him. Perhaps it was, in fact, the shortest distance.

David's son, Solomon, later recorded this jewel of wisdom: "Trust in the Lord with all your heart, and do not lean on your own understanding. In all your ways acknowledge Him, and He will make straight your paths" (Proverbs 3:5–6, ESV).

Discussion

Though I call and cry for help, He shuts out my prayer; He has blocked my ways with blocks of stones; He has made my paths crooked. (Lamentations 3:8–9, ESV) Do you ever feel like that? Are you in the middle of such a path right now?

Why might God not allow us to see the map of where He is taking us?

When has the Lord caused you to alter course and you later realized it was the best route?

For Further Reading

Proverbs 16:1–4, 9, Isaiah 42:16, Isaiah 55:8–9, Romans 8:28

#

Dressed and Ready to Go

Anytime we invite a non-sailor to join us for a sail, inevitably the question comes: *what should I wear?*

Similarly, a new sailor needs to know appropriate apparel for sailing—particularly in weather. There are two important factors: stay warm and stay dry.

There is an old sailing adage that says there is no such thing as bad weather, only bad clothes. Foul weather gear is essential. The coat and pants must be waterproof and warm. They must keep the rain from running down your arms while raising a sail. They must have reflectors so you can be seen at night. Waterproof shoes or boots that grip are vital in foul weather.

Other considerations:

- Quick dry, breathable clothing that is easy to maneuver in
- UV protection—sunscreen, sunglasses, or maybe a hat
- Perhaps sailing gloves to protect hands for working the sheets
- PFDs for safety

Shoes are extremely important—they must grip, not slip. On Teleo, we have a rule: no flip-flops. (We have a friend who broke her back on a sailboat due to flip flops.) Close-toed shoes are safest, and no black soled shoes to scuff up the boat!

Did You Know?

Chesapeake watermen have traditionally worn a sou'wester hat during foul weather. The brim and elongated back of these hats act as a gutter, draining water off the back while keeping the neck dry. Dave receives much ribbing from his wife and friends when he wears his sou'wester hat. But he stays dry!

Statue of a waterman wearing a traditional sou'wester hat at
The Sailing Emporium in Rock Hall, Maryland.
Photo courtesy of Sandy McGetrick.

Key Scripture

Put on the full armor of God.

(EPHESIANS 6:11A, ESV)

...put on the new self, which is being renewed in knowledge in the image of its Creator...as God's chosen people, holy and dearly loved, clothe yourselves with compassion, kindness, humility, gentleness and patience.

(COLOSSIANS 3:10, 12, ESV)

Just as a new sailor has a bit of clothes shopping to do, so in a much more beautiful and deeper sense, a new Christian receives new "clothing" at the point of salvation—the clothing of Christ.

The Bible teaches that when we become a Christian, we become a new creation. And as we grow in Him, we are being renewed further into His likeness. Often, in order to define this in simple ways for us to understand, scripture uses the metaphor of clothing.

So what is the armor of God? The belt of *truth*, the breastplate of *righteousness*, shoes fitted for the readiness that comes from the *Gospel of peace*, a shield of *faith*, the helmet of *salvation*, and the sword of the *Spirit* which is the *Word*. It is important to note: none of this is my armor; it is all God's!

When I became a Christian, an important transaction took place. Christ wore my sin on the cross and gave me His righteousness. When the Father looks at me, He sees Jesus. Jesus clothes me with His clothes—who He is.

Discussion

Do you struggle to believe that when God looks at you, He sees the righteousness of His Son?

What other attributes of Christ do we wear as we become more like Him?

Have you personally experienced the transaction of exchanging your sin for His righteousness?

For Further Reading

2 Corinthians 5:21, Isaiah 61:10, Galatians 3:26–27, Ephesians 6:10–18

#

Teamwork

While it is possible to enjoy a day sail by yourself, it is wise to sail as a team on longer passages. It also makes sense to carefully choose and vary your team.

One person might be a better navigator. One person is a better sailor. One person knows how to troubleshoot mechanical problems. One person might be a better cook. One person might be very cautious and one more of a risk-taker. One person knows weather.

The key is to combine all these talents to inform the captain—the ultimate decision-maker. It is also important that the crew submit to the captain as indecision or insubordination is often more dangerous than a less than optimal decision.

Key Scripture

We are to grow up in every way into Him who is the head, into Christ, from whom the whole body, joined and held together by every joint with which it is equipped, when each part is working properly, makes the body grow so that it builds itself up in love.

(EPHESIANS 4:15–16, ESV)

It is a humbling thought, this truth that as Christians we are the body of Christ. He remains the head, our Captain, and we become his hands and feet to do His kingdom work on this earth. The Bible is clear that at the point of salvation, God gives us gifts. We call these spiritual gifts. In a healthy church body, members are actively serving with the gifts God gave them. An eye is not attempting to be a hand, a hand is not expecting a foot to join him as a hand, and a mouth is not mute. Each is using their gift and valuing all other gifts just as crucial. When a church body is healthy, at least three things are true about its members:

1. They are looking to their Head first, not each other. They are trusting in Captain Jesus, following His Word, and submitting to His authority.
2. They are loving one another. Jesus said that the world will know we are His disciples if we love one another. Love is going to produce selfless harmony when serving together as a team, and that will cause others to take note.
3. They are using their gifts faithfully. Members who do not serve in their divine sweet spot are going to burn out. This sometimes happens because members who have that gift choose not to serve, and others fill the void. A healthy church is serving in their giftedness.

Discussion

Do you know your spiritual gift?

What are some of the talents, passions, and traits that God has given you?

Can you think of ways you can serve the Lord and others using those divine gifts?

For Further Reading

Romans 12:3–8, 1 Corinthians 12:4–7, 14–20

\#

Psalm 107

Some went down to the sea in ships,
doing business on the great waters;
they saw the deeds of the Lord,
his wondrous works in the deep.
For he commanded and raised the stormy wind,
which lifted up the waves of the sea.

They mounted up to heaven; they went down to the depths;
their courage melted away in their evil plight;
they reeled and staggered like drunken men
and were at their wits' end.

Then they cried to the Lord in their trouble,
and he delivered them from their distress.
He made the storm be still,
and the waves of the sea were hushed.
Then they were glad that the waters were quiet,
and he brought them to their desired haven.

Let them thank the Lord for his steadfast love,
for his wondrous works to the children of man!

(Psalm 107:23–31, ESV)

\#

HALYARDS AND LINES

An experienced sailor distinguishes when a sound is out of place and investigates. It might be that the boat is pointed too close to the wind or a sail is incompletely hoisted, trimmed, or maybe not properly fastened or sheeted. Loose sails and loose cords require intervention by the skipper or crew.

There are two types of rigging on sailboats. *Running rigging* is comprised of all the lines that form the controls for sailing. There are no ropes on sailboats, only lines of various types—each with a name and purpose. The lines used to hoist sails are called halyards, while the lines used to trim (to tighten/bring in or loosen/let out) the sails are called sheets. So if the main halyard is flapping and making noise, the main sail is not fully raised. If the jib sheets are loose, the boat is either too close to the wind or the sheet is not properly tightened.

Standing rigging are the stronger lines, typically core or cables that support the mast to hold it upright: forestays and backstays run front and back and shrouds to the sides.

Any rigging checklist will include inspections for misalignment, cracks, rust, corrosion, bends, leaks, broken strands of wire, and indications of stress. While it is most important to find the big stuff, it is equally important to pull out the magnifying glass and look for the small stuff like cables starting to fray or rust.

Rig failure, like hull integrity and steering/rudder failure, will completely disable a vessel as it removes all source of power to sail in a given direction. What may start out small can eventually become catastrophic.

Key Scripture

Your cords hang loose; they cannot hold the mast firm in its place or keep the sail spread out.

(ISAIAH 33:23A, ESV)

The key scripture is a picture of God's people experiencing total rig failure. They are a disabled ship, adrift at sea, without power.

In the Bible, the sea is often represented as a place of "restless evil." One can well imagine how, in its mystery, the sea frightened even ancient mariners, who did not fully understand it. And even now, though we understand more, a disabled ship is a dangerous thing. It is not only about the vessel, it's about what that loss of vessel could mean—loss of life.

So in this analogy, God's broken people are then not only crippled but vulnerable to further catastrophe. How did they get there?

At the very least, it starts with the small stuff. Lack of inspection—daily confession—and little cracks widen into bigger ones. Sin has a ripple effect in our lives. It impacts our relationship with God and how we view ourselves, our relations with others, and even our relation to creation itself as it can harm our physical well-being. Sin tears us apart and, when it is full blown, will utterly wreck a life.

But there is hope. God heals the brokenhearted and binds their wounds. In that same passage, God is pictured as the Lord in majesty protecting us from the majestic enemy ships blocking our way. He is our Judge, our Lawgiver, our King, and our Savior. And at the point that our cords hang loose with the mast falling off because of our own sin, inattention, and recklessness, He forgives our iniquity.

Discussion

James 1:15 talks about small sins that when fully grown can bring about death. Can you think of an example of how that might happen?

Do you know God as your Protector, Judge, Lawgiver, King, and Savior? Does one of those titles of God leap out at you personally?

For Further Reading

James 1:13–15, 1 John 1:9, Isaiah 33:21–24

#

RUDDER

Equestrians know that a small bit in the horse's mouth will allow the rider to turn the great beast in whatever direction he wants to go.

In a sailboat that equivalent is the rudder.

The rudder is a flat blade near the stern of a boat connected vertically beneath the ship's tiller or wheel. Its primary purpose is to steer the boat, but in order for that to work properly, water must be moving past the rudder. In other words, the ship must be "making way." Often first time sailors will comment after taking the helm that you can feel the power of the harnessed wind on the rudder.

(As a sidenote, if you like that feeling, you are about to spend a lot of money buying and maintaining sailboats!)

A balanced boat with sails properly set will be easier to steer and put less strain on the rudder. An imbalanced boat will be more difficult to steer and can become tiring for the helmsman.

A rudder failure at sea is a very serious situation, perhaps second only to a fire aboard, for the rudder is necessary to steer the boat whether under sail or power. Without it, the ship is mostly helpless although there are some "approximate" ways to steer using sails or dragging objects behind to pull the boat in one direction or another. None of these are as good as a functioning rudder.

It is amazing to see a great ship out of water and notice how small the rudder is that steers the ship. It is a fraction of the size of the hull yet holds the power to guide the entire ship in the desired direction.

Key Scripture

Look at the ships also: though they are so large and are driven by strong winds, they are guided by a very small rudder wherever the will of the pilot directs. So also the tongue is a small member, yet it boasts of great things.

(JAMES 3:4–5, ESV)

James 3:1–12 gives context to this key scripture. Like a rudder, the tongue wields great power. When outside forces press in—whether challenging circumstances or difficult people—the tongue has the potential to swoop in and do either great harm or good. The very words that come out of a person's mouth have the power to alter those circumstances. Those words can guide an entire situation into a new direction, for better or worse. Words have tremendous power with lasting effects to both wound and heal.

The childish saying "Sticks and stones may break my bones, but words can never hurt me" is false. Better to trip over a rock and break a bone than to experience the betrayal, gossip, or slander by the words of another. It's an easy bet that healing comes far more quickly for the former. And how many times do we long to take our words back, knowing they've inflicted pain on the recipient of our outburst?

"...no human being can tame the tongue... with it we bless our Lord and Father, and with it we curse people who are made in the likeness of God" (James 3:8–9, ESV). Note: *All* are made in the image of God.

While no human being may tame the tongue, God does sanctify His children, giving us a Helper through the Holy Spirit, cleansing us of unrighteousness—including our mouths.

Discussion

Do you struggle to control your tongue?

Is there someone you need to forgive or ask for forgiveness?

For Further Reading

Proverbs 18:21, Luke 6:45, Matthew 5:23–24, Ephesians 4:29, Psalm 73:21–26, Psalm 19:12–14

#

Evidence of the Invisible

Most people don't think about the wind as part of daily life. It might cross our minds when we see the devastation caused by a storm on the news; otherwise, it has relatively little impact on our modern lives.

But this is not true for the typical sailor. A sailor sees the factory smoke blowing in the direction of the wind. He sees the flag hanging limp. He sees ducks on a pond or birds on posts pointed into the wind to allow them stability and lift for takeoff.

Although wind is invisible, it is the power source for the sailboat, and understanding it can make a journey fast, comfortable, and safe or slow, unpleasant, and potentially risky.

Sailors use information they gather about the wind to draw conclusions such as the following:

- How to set the sails to take maximum advantage of the wind to reach the desired destination.
- How small ripples on the water in the distance indicate an approaching gust of wind.
- What type of sail configuration to use and when to shorten sail based on the speed of the wind. Wind speed translates into power on an exponential pace.

- When changes to wind can be expected. For example, as a cold front passes, winds will back (move counterclockwise) and then veer (move clockwise) with stronger winds.
- The effect of nearby land which can cause strong channeling winds through valleys, confused winds ("dirty air") next to large objects, land and sea breezes.

Key Scripture

For His invisible attributes, namely, His eternal power and divine nature, have been clearly perceived, ever since the creation of the world, in the things that have been made.

(ROMANS 1:20, ESV)

Have you ever experienced the awe of the invisible, feeling the wind's power in the tiller of a sloop? That is what first hooked us to sailing, feeling the unseen wind in our hands. The wind itself is invisible, yet no person would doubt its existence because we see its effects—flapping flags, swaying trees, and silent boats gliding over water.

We must think of God that way. He is invisible, but we cannot doubt His existence when we consider the wonder of His creation—evident by all that is seen and felt. Perhaps this truth is most clearly demonstrated in creation by human life itself. "The Lord God formed the man...and breathed into his nostrils the breath of life, and the man became a living being" (Genesis 2:7, ESV). The mystery of life can become so commonplace that we lose sight of our Creator, yet life is the miracle we live with every day. The big question is why?

"He (Christ) is the image of the invisible God, the firstborn over all creation. For by Him all things were created: things in heaven and on earth, visible and invisible... all things were created by Him and for Him" (Colossians 1:15–16, ESV). Simply put, we were created for Christ.

But this is not all! As the image of the invisible God, Christ Himself is the best evidence of God's existence since He is God seen by human eyes. "Christ died for our sins... He was buried... He was raised on the third day... He appeared to Peter, and then to the Twelve. After that, He appeared to more than five hundred of the brothers at the same time" (1 Corinthians 15:3–6, ESV). Over 500 people were eyewitnesses to the resurrection of Christ!

The great mathematician, Blaise Pascal, pointed out that we marvel at the birth of a baby yet remain unconvinced that one could rise from the dead. Which is harder to accomplish?

Discussion

What are other ways we experience the evidence of God in creation?

#

PSALM 19

The heavens declare the glory of God,
And the sky above proclaims His handiwork.
Day to day pours out speech,
And night to night reveals knowledge.
There is no speech, nor are there words,
Whose voice is not heard.
Their voice goes out through all the earth,
And their words to the end of the world.
In them He has set a tent for the sun,
Which comes out like a bridegroom leaving His chamber,
And, like a strong man, runs its course with joy.
Its rising is from the end of the heavens,
And its circuit to the end of them,
And there is nothing hidden from its heat.

The law of the Lord is perfect, reviving the soul;
The testimony of the Lord is sure, making wise the simple;
The precepts of the Lord are right, rejoicing the heart;
The commandment of the Lord is pure, enlightening the eyes;
The fear of the Lord is clean, enduring forever;
The rules of the Lord are true, and righteous altogether.
More to be desired are they than gold, even much fine gold;

Sweeter also than honey and drippings of the honeycomb.
Moreover, by them is your servant warned;
In keeping them there is great reward.

(Psalm 19:1–11, ESV)

#

RULES OF THE ROAD

Just like traffic laws for automobiles, rules govern the interaction of vessels on the water, establishing a consistent way to navigate safely and avoid collisions. Water is a little more complicated than highways in that there are not lines or traffic lights; furthermore, none of the vessels have brakes. So it is important for boaters to understand the rules of the road for everyone's safety. Nothing is more daunting than for a small sailboat capable of going five knots to be overtaken by a ship that is a quarter of a mile long and requires five miles to stop. Modern technologies to enable ship-to-ship communications (Radar, VHF, and AIS) have helped to reduce the risk but are no substitute for following the rules.

Most often sailboats have courtesies over powerboats. That basically means that powerboats have the responsibility to avoid a sailboat. However that is not always true. Sailboats with the motor running are considered a powerboat. Also there are numerous power vessels with special conditions that make them higher in priority on the list than sailboats. For example, it could be a vessel that is in distress or dead in the water. Or perhaps a large freighter that can only find adequate depth particular channel requires sailboats to stay clear.

LIVING IN THE DESIGN

Some of the most complicated applications of the rules come about when two sailboats meet at a "crossing" which really means they are on a collision course. Each vessel has a responsibility. One vessel is required to "stand on," meaning to maintain course and speed. The other vessel is required to "give way," meaning it must take a pronounced evasive action. Knowing which boat is which depends on other factors such as tack (port vs. starboard) and nearness to wind direction (windward vs. leeward).

The US Coast Guard Navigation Rules booklet explains it all.

Key Scripture

So then, the word of the LORD to them will become: Do this, do that, a rule for this, a rule for that; a little here, a little there—so that as they go they will fall backward....

(ISAIAH 28:13, NIV)

For all who rely on works of the law are under a curse; for it is written, 'Cursed be everyone who does not abide by all things written in the Book of the Law, and do them.'

(GALATIANS 3:10, ESV)

The Law was given by God, and it was necessary to teach knowledge of sin, to put words to a moral right and wrong, and to establish the impossible God-sized standard. It was never meant to be a savior.

Yet we are so often given to keeping the rules as a religion or a way to earn the Lord's favor. Humans are wired as worker-bees. We either frantically work, work, and work to achieve, or we thumb our noses at the impossible rules and rebel. One shows up as legalism, and the other as a false freedom to sin. Neither saves nor sanctifies.

Jesus taught us to enter by the narrow gate, for wide is the gate that leads to destruction. Rebels get their back up at that, while legalists either feel guilty or try all the harder (or both), for narrow implies to our minds something difficult and judgmental.

And yet how impossible it would be to keep every rule demanded in the wide gate, while the narrow gate is not a rule at all! It is one Person: Jesus Christ. He is the way, the truth, and the life; no one goes to the Father but by Him. And how do we enter through Jesus the Narrow Gate? By faith alone.

We trust in our Savior, and *then* His Spirit within helps us to obey. Neither the obedience nor the commandments do the saving, only Jesus.

Discussion

Do your interactions with God tend to be more of a religion (earning His favor) or relationship (accepting His grace)?

For Further Reading

Matthew 15:8–9, John 10:7–11, Romans 3:20–23, 8:1–4, Galatians 5:1

#

TIME TO SHORTEN SAIL

"Once you've realized it's time to reef, it's too late"
(SAILING ADAGE)

To reef means to shorten sail. Reducing sail area is the appropriate response to an approaching storm or high winds.

Appropriate may not sound fun. We well know the temptation to delay reefing and eek out as much of that full sail as possible. But reefing will allow the helmsman to maintain control of the boat thereby reducing the danger of broaching or capsizing.

And if you are a risk-taker who couldn't care less about the "appropriate" response, consider this: reefing in heavy winds will also improve the boat's performance, diminishing excessive heel and drag.

So when do you shorten sail? The short answer is before you think you need to. Anticipating bad weather is key as it is very difficult and dangerous to reef once the vessel is overpowered.

Check the forecast, have a weather radio on board, and watch the skies. Is there a small craft advisory? Put in a reef. Are white-cap conditions ahead? Put in a reef. Are other boats in that same direction heeled significantly over? Time to reef.

The better prepared you are, the safer and better your boat will sail.

Did You Know?

The power of wind is exponential. For example, one might conclude that a ten-knot wind is twice as strong as a five-knot wind, but it is not.

It is four times as strong.

Key Scripture

For He says, 'In a favorable time I listened to you, and in a day of salvation I have helped you.' Behold, now is the favorable time; behold, now is the day of salvation.

(2 CORINTHIANS 6:2, ESV)

Do we know the favorable time of salvation? Are we ready? Jesus addressed these questions again and again. In the parable of the wedding feast (Luke 12 below) and in the parable of the ten virgins (Matthew 25), Jesus is the bridegroom for those who are ready.

Jesus is lovingly seeking His people, but so often we close our hearts to that call. The Christians we know might seem boring. A life of obedience might seem demanding. We eek out that last bit of "fun" and take the risk that we could make it to a death-bed decision. We play Russian roulette with the God who says strongly, "Behold, *now* is the favorable time; behold *now* is the day of salvation."

Some might delay that pull so long that they fear it is too late. The parable of the vineyard in Matthew 20 is a beautiful picture of people receiving Jesus at all stages of life. The one who calls on the name of the Lord at 6:00 pm at 9:00 pm and even in the eleventh hour will be saved. Of the latter, we have the thief on the cross as an example for us. The thief reefed his sail, as it were, in that last moment before capsizing. If you have breath in your lungs, it is not too late.

But be prepared. Nobody knows what tomorrow brings; an opportunity for a deathbed conversion is no guarantee. For those who reef in the morning, what a glorious sail it is. Do not listen to the whispered lie that pleasure is in the danger and joy is in the world. Though life in Christ is not without challenges or suffering, it is true joy. "In Your presence there is fullness of joy... [and] pleasures forevermore" (Psalm 16:11, ESV).

Discussion

What is the appropriate time to live for Christ?

What does the world tell us about why we should wait?

For Further Reading

Luke 12:35–40, Matthew 25:1–13, Matthew 20:1–16, Luke 23:39–43, Revelation 3:20, John 1:12

#

REDEMPTION

There is something romantic about an old wooden schooner. One can imagine the boat in her glory days—perfectly appointed, designed with the utmost care and gliding effortlessly across the open seas.

As time passes, however, the lovely ship begins to wear the weathered "skin" of her old captain. Storms and hard use strip away her beauty and then her function until she is forced to retire from the sea.

The old schooner is consigned to a forgotten corner of a boatyard or, worse still, stripped apart. If she is lucky, she remains in the water alongside some dock. She might even take on a different purpose as a museum. But she no longer lives the purpose for which she was originally designed. She has become a sailboat which does not (or cannot) sail.

Everyone loves a story about a sailor who finds just such a boat—well beyond her sailing days—and lovingly restores her to her former glory. In the final scene, the sailor is shown at the helm letting the boat do what she was designed to do and rediscovering her lost glory.

Key Scripture

If anyone is in Christ, he is a new creation.

(2 CORINTHIANS 5:17, ESV)

In the beginning, we were something like that "newborn" beautifully appointed schooner—only we were lovingly designed by our Creator *in His own image* and *for His glory*. God called us His workmanship, the crown of His creation, and we walked with Him in the garden. Out of all creation, we had an intimate relationship with the Lord.

But foolishly, we turned our back on God and chose dry rot for our souls—the dry rot of sin—and from then on we lived in a fallen world of sin, suffering, death, and separation from our perfect Designer. How many times have we felt forgotten, stripped apart, and empty—not living the purpose for which we were designed?

At the very point of our sin, right there in the garden, God set a plan in motion for our redemption. We could not save ourselves. We could not rid our own dry rot, any more than an old schooner could restore itself. No amount of "doing good" could cure the sin within; God said even our righteous deeds were as filthy rags. Our only hope was God Himself—for the One who designed us in His own image was the only One who could restore us.

So God in Christ entered human history. While we were still sinners, God showed His great love for us by dying on a cross. Through his death on our behalf, Christ redeemed us out of sin and into a relationship with Him. The separation was gone! Christ not only redeemed and restored us, but adopted us as children to share in His inheritance of eternal life—completely free of sin, pain, and death.

In Christ is our redemption. In Christ, God makes all things new. In Christ, we live in the design of who God created us to be.

Discussion

What is the story of redemption in your life?

Who do you know that is in need of redemption?

For Further Reading

Genesis 1:26–31, Exodus 6:3–9, Isaiah 50:2, 59:1–2, 59:15–16, Galatians 4:4–5, Ephesians 2:8–10, 4:24

#

ACKNOWLEDGMENTS

We are both grateful to our parents, Jim and Melody Evans and Bob and Audrey Stadler, who instilled in us our mutual love of boating at an early age. We each have cherished memories of summers spent at Lake Viking, the Current River, and the Lake of the Ozarks in the landlocked state of Missouri.

To grown children, Matt and Cait, who have patiently listened to us talk about boats, sailing, and this project, and who have embellished many a boating tale at family gatherings! We love your humor, and we love you.

To John Bregel who gave Dave his first sailing experience on Hoover Reservoir in Columbus, Ohio.

Our dear friend, Captain Mike Brown (owner of Captain in You Sailing Schools, Inc.), for the countless discussions on obscure sailing topics and our sailing adventures on lakes, the Chesapeake, and the Caribbean.

We are grateful to our many teachers, in particular, Captain Joe Kliment who taught us bareboat chartering in the Virgin Islands and who, along with his wife, Ruth, reviewed and edited the technical aspects of sailing within this book. Also, Captain Tom Tursi of The Maryland School of Sailing & Seamanship who taught us many aspects of navigation.

A special thank you to Dorie Thompson for her input in

formatting and structuring the devotional and to Rich and Marilyn Hansen for their many helpful comments and encouragement in the latter stages of this project.

To Amy Nelson of Roaring Jellyfish Designs for the design of our Teleo logo.

We wish to acknowledge our many sailing friends, too many to mention without leaving someone out, in particular, our friends at the Nockamixon Sail Club and Rock Hall Sailing Club and Parkview friends at The Sailing Emporium, the Annapolis Yacht Club, and EP Sailing Ministries at the Evangelical Presbyterian Church of Annapolis.

Finally, we acknowledge our Lord and Savior Jesus Christ, who created, loved, and redeemed us for His glory. We offer this book up to Him. "Not to us, O Lord, not to us, but to Your name goes all the glory for Your unfailing love and Your faithfulness!" (Psalm 115:1, NLT).